The Tower

Also by John Egan and published by Ginninderra Press
Lines Continue Forever
The Long Way Home
Crossing the Heads
Reworkings (Pocket Poets)
Reworkings 2 (Pocket Poets)
Reworkings 3 (Pocket Poets)
Reworkings 4 (Pocket Poets)
Reworkings 5 (Pocket Poets)
Sydney Central (Pocket Poets)
Play It Louder (Pocket Poets)
Putting to Sea (Pocket Poets)
A Safe Harbour (Pocket Poets)
Visions (Pocket Poets)
Swans (Pocket Poets)
Mischief Eyes (Pocket Poets)
Dreams of Butterflies (Pocket Poets)
Red Roses (Pocket Poets)

With Brenda Eldridge
An Unexpected Harmony (Pocket Poets)

John Egan

The Tower

Acknowledgements

Some of these poems first appeared in *The Mozzie*, *Positive Words*, *The Write Angle*, *Beyond the Rainbow*, *Tamba*, *Polestar*, *The Valley Micropress*, *FreeXpression*, *Yellow Moon*, *House Happenings*, *Poetry Matters*, *Page Seventeen*, *Pendulum*, *Tarralla*, *Staples*, *Ripples*, *House Happenings* and *Five Bells*.

'Tightrope Walking, First, Illawarra Writers Centre Circus Risky Poetry Competition, 2006

'A Suburb', First, Coal Creek Poetry Competition, 2017

For Maurice (Morrie) Egan (1923–2007), my father

The Tower
ISBN 978 1 76041 567 9
Copyright © text John Egan 2018
Cover photo: St Mary's Cathedral © Fyle
Author photo: Peter Egan

First published 2018 by
GINNINDERRA PRESS
PO Box 3461 Port Adelaide 5015
www.ginninderrapress.com.au

Contents

Tightrope Walking	11
The Tower	13
St Mary's, Sydney	15
St Augustine's, Balmain	16
Romanesque	17
The Broadway Site	18
Skeletons of Air	19
Berlei House	20
Dangar Terrace	22
Performance	24
Green City	25
Patterns	26
Snake	28
Sets His Course	30
Perspectives	31
A White Horse	33
If at First…	34
Alessandro and the Giant Bird	35
The Edge of Reality	37
From Nothing	38
Space, Matter, Time	39
The Goldilocks Zone	41
Vertigo	43
Optimism	44
Parallels Never Meet	45
The Mountain Train	46
Post-traumatic	48
Recollections	49
Stars	50
A Pebble	51

Early Spring	52
Vapour Trails	53
The Waves	54
Spring Rain	55
Silence	56
Autumn to May	57
A White Mug	58
The Magician	59
Ghostly	60
Ghostwalking	61
Faces in the Sea	63
The Night	64
The Young Moon	65
Dangerous	66
Coalcliff	67
Illawarra Dreaming	69
The Gardens	71
A Suburb	72
Gliding Home	73
Over the Shoalhaven	75
Driving Home 3 a.m.	76
Race the Storm	77
Driving Home	78
Home	79
Our House	80
Spirit of Place	81
Rocks and Water	83
'Tramps and Hawkers'	85
Something	87
Muse	88
Wrecking Ball	89
My Desk	90

A Silhouette	91
Angels in the Mind	92
The Imp	94
Special	95
Whatever Remains	96
Autumn 1994	97
Great Rainbow, Dad	98
Gosford Hospital, 2 a.m.	100
My Father's Rainbow	102
Haunted	103
For Destruction Ice	104
A Touch	105
Six Months Later	106
Ern Malley's Children	107
Common Sense, Really	108
Malvolio Again	109
Diligence	110
Choose Your Ground	111
Stormcloud	112
Leaves in the City	113
Milkman	114
Rowena	115
Long Black Hair	117
No Ordinary Lunch	119
Waiting for Discharge	120
Eighteen Kilometres	122
Jervis Bay	125
Lives	126
Then and Since and Now	127
Waiting	128
Hear and Do Not Hear	131
A Problem of Intelligence	133

Conservatives Rule Okay	135
The Future and Bone	136
The Mirror	138
Left and Right	139
How to Break the Law in Ten Easy Steps	140
Parents	141
It Could Have Been Here	143
The Greenland Colonies	146

I pace upon the battlements and stare
On the foundations of a house, or where
Tree, like a sooty finger, starts from the earth;
And send imagination forth…

        W.B. Yeats, 'The Tower'

Tightrope Walking

The blank page silent
like a chasm
and there is no net.

The blue Parker
your only wire
to safety
or into space.

Measure its weight
balanced on your fingers,
across the hollow
of your thumb.

Words flower
like geometry, inch onto wires
taut with print,
syllables like nerves.

Phrases cling to your flesh,
toes and feet test each vowel,
consonants. like vertigo,
the abyss between each line.

The poem explodes
as applause
rolling up,
open mouths, breathless faces

and your eyes transfixed
by that still point
in the void,

the nothing
you didn't know
you were even
aiming for.

The Tower

Rounded arches, Italianate windows,
the setting sun strikes the tower.
Its stones are glowing, the final
reflections of the day.

Not the yellow white of sandstone
in the midday glare, nor the grey-melt blue
of late evening, but pink and red,
the crazy colours of mild sunlight.

Never the same tower. Every new hour
it changes, a beacon for the seasons,
radiates summer heat, warmth in the cool
and burns with cold in the ice-shards

of wind and rain, deters your touch
as if it exists merely to look beautiful
and provide nothing of use or comfort,
a mannequin who parades exquisite fashion.

Shadows are thrown across the lawn,
the gasp of chill, when half a year ago
the shade was longed for, its cool breath
to soothe a furnace of sweat and summer.

Stand on the opposite side of the bay
and the tower rises from a green canopy,
dominates a mere of water
like a castle protecting villages,

but is ever the enemy of still water
whose colours only copy the sunlight and clouds,
while the tower absorbs them all
and everything becomes its day.

St Mary's, Sydney

A canyon chiselled by giants.
Gothic arches, pillars and bays
march forward, over the high altar,
purple now in Lent, where the Great North Window
glows in quatrefoils of light.

Pillars stand three storeys, shoulders of stone,
layered stepwork, arcade and clerestory
that build to four monumental arches
where nave and transept cross in collision.

Fluted, liana-like in coils, bunched in
jungle overgrowth, high trunks and branches
flow in stone, an edifice that gestures
to the sky-god, to an airy heaven,
though built in stone, stubbornly hugs the ground.
Tree-forms cling in the nave and aisles, earthbound
in horizontals like a cave.

Some sit, some kneel and pray, most wander,
pious tourists, pilgrims in hush and awe
cast into tangible quiet, sensuous
reverence, this sculpting of elementals,
space and stone and light, red and blue light-rays
of stained glass that pierce the darkness
like God's fingers reaching the forest floor,
full signatures of distant stars at night,
the carved canyons of masonry and faith.

St Augustine's, Balmain

From the east the church dominates the sky
with its tower on the hill, Italian,
almost medieval, a neat suburb below
sweeping away like a town walled in water.

Yet approach from the west, walk across the park,
and it's a small doorway in a leafy street,
a red brick sanctuary beyond the school,
unassuming, suburban, very quiet.

Inside is nothing much, an altar, the lamp
and its confession of light and emptiness.
Yet here's the thin touch stirs all power, all life.
The hand of God depends on where you look.

Romanesque

This derelict, old Tooth's brewery site
sprawls across this end of Chippendale.
Its bricks protect a decayed street
and outer buildings form defensive walls.

Inwards, like some ancient, mellow fortress, sheer
ramparts of the glazed, brown-surfaced brick
imply the solid, plain integrity
of industrial function, grace and style.

A warehouse shades a cross of narrow lanes,
rows of terrace houses peel and squat below
this elegant, grand facade, an empty building's
formal face, majestic and symmetrical.

Eight piers, a cornice and a pediment,
arches on the ground floor windows and a base
for matching towers of decorated brick.
This early Federation Warehouse Style

inspires a spirit from the Middle Ages
in the sombre permanence of Romanesque,
reflects a staid Edwardian quietness in
this century's frenzied, inner-city din.

The Broadway Site

Look down the length of Outram Street,
mellowed walls and factory brick, demolished
now. New emptiness disturbs the eye.
There's little left to focus on.

Only the vacant sky and cluttered valley
unfold against tight, spindled towers.
The brittle stones of the university
float along their ridge, expose the sun.

Neo-gothic dreamings, far abstractions.
No tactile sensuousness in what is here.
No mysteries brew where the warehouse aged with time.
No mystery in distance or in space

Beyond a temporary, unkempt fence,
bleeding the skyline and the street
a concrete-whitened landscape withdraws beneath
endless battalions of dumb, featureless air.

Skeletons of Air

Slim skeletons hinged across the sky.
Latticeworks of bone stride across rooftops,
reach down to fuss on building sites
like tall fathers, then swing in dizzy arcs
of thinnest air and pirouette like dancers
laced in steel, balanced merely by the wind.

Seedlings ride in their long palms, planted
precisely where the strangest gardens grow,
blossoms of apartments and office blocks
nurtured by the skeletons of giants
that circle like anxious parents
busy above us in the bony sky.

Berlei House

The space flowing in,
huge windows front and back,
steps from Regent Street.
The panorama Central Station
and the cluttered skyline Surry Hills.
The wider view rises up
to Sydney University, the valley
under Chippendale, a laneway
Goold Street to the rear.

Inter-war, Chicago style,
1925. A facade
that's understated, clean,
symmetrical.
Elaboration of a cornice
almost to a pediment
the fifth and upper storey.
Broad, emphatic spandrels
climbing from the street.
It's more, of course, the atmosphere
that the style invokes.
Inside, it's intimate,
relaxed and cool. The elements
are built to human scale
in harmony of wall and space.
In a word – its comfortable.

Textures, ratios, proportions
all set against the dominant,
round, internal columns,
precise, disciplined,
defining every floor –
the strength we work beside
and in relation to.

But now we're moving out
to the tramp of workmen
building, moving, dividing
so blue and sand are changed
to cream and green, new walls appear
and some just go
but the building's got good bones,
there's structure beneath the neat,
the merely superficial.
If buildings can develop souls
through years of use
and permanence, a slow seepage
of mysteries, their decades of life,
the times of those
who only come and go,
then this old building
already has a gentle one.

Dangar Terrace

A row of seven
late-Victorian terrace houses.
I look for you in everything that's wonderful.
I see symmetry focused
on the cornice of the central house
and at each end shops like castles.

I see you in a gown of silver grey,
your shoulders vulnerable as wings.

The facade curves to a major road
and a lane I've crossed so many times
and never noticed how the shadows fall
from balconies and wrought-iron rusts,
submissive in the sun.

Traffic slides in routine.
Café diners sip their coffee.
They do not feel your eyes
among the mirrors nor watch you
lift your hair to tie it
nor mark the sadness in your face
as we say goodbye.

I see you naked and in chains
waiting.

I walk towards you.
The building captures you,
beautiful, intense and holds you like a prisoner
inside a tower,
as if bewildered
by a fantasy
fading into real.

Performance

Again November,
brazen jacarandas
flaunt their flowers

in a floor show of mauve,
unashamed, brilliant,
their carpets of petals

like clothes they've scattered
across the floor –
showgirls and strippers,

raucous and glamorous,
whirlpools of feathers and silk,
stark in the spotlit sun,

a backdrop of green suburbs,
dark applause and cheers
from audience, drinkers, doorways.

Cool in the heat
as the seasons revolve
to bare skin and summer,

the trees undress
in chorus lines,
burlesque in the late spring.

Green City

In the city, at street level,
you can miss the trees. The largest
evergreen stands strangely invisible
just a brown trunk arrayed among
files and ranks of poles, the street signs:
Bus Zone, No Parking, No Standing.
Tell that to the trees. Eye level,
they can exist but seem not there at all.

But look up and there's a green world,
an attic storey of foliage
and branches, a sky of forest
and green aquariums of filtered light.
We scurry around the feet of giants.

In pure forests, leaves, bark and branches drop,
build up, litter the ground for centuries,
fallen trunks rotting among mounds of time,
homes for animals, ground and shrub and nest dwellers.
You can't walk there, entanglements
of thrust and growth, renewal, rich decay,
the thrive of another kind of city.

They say forests are not individual trees
but societies that communicate
and organise themselves along their roots,
transmit their nutrients through soil and rain.
Each tree is a part of the complete whole,
like cities underground, the forest floor,
their crowns and canopies ranged in the sky.

Patterns

Le Corbusier or a pattern by Mondrian.
It's geometric.
From the library window
look down at foreground foliage and branch,
the zap of traffic whipped through
interstices between the leaves.

Look ahead
at cream symmetry, horizontal,
the two-storeyed wall
of shops below their flats and storage –
pediment and parapet, gable and bow windows,
dignified construction of the '20s,
a building of style and proportion.

Look up, beyond the pediment,
new high-rise: apartments
and balconies, south-facing slits
of windows, the greys,
the browns and creams of high, clean walls,
a square turret like a fortress,
the Norman castle keep imposed
on low-rise town and street.

Above, the crane's impressive almost T,
90 degrees, set-square latticework,
steel verticals, patterned lifts and webs
of horizontal grid narrows
as it reaches over the new building,
guards and comforts, echoes
the length of the older building,
its repetition a stripe, the formality
of God's right arm on the seventh day.

Beyond, the sweet emptiness of sky,
pure and clear at evening, though crossed
by thin, insistent diagonals,
intrusive falls, planes that trespass
against all the artist's intentions
whose aim and passage disturb
his balance, unsettle his parallels
like paint drops splashed on a wall,
they appear, keep moving down, then vanish.

Snake

I've never touched a snake.
Arboreal creature, camouflaged
against the branches that you twine around.
Innocent birds see you only
as part of the tree, matched
by shadow and leaves, but now
you're pressed into coils,
                            now you flow
across our veranda, one metre, two,
perhaps more, harmless but hypnotic
in myth, satanic, the snake
of legend invading our home.

Fascinating your curse,
as if from caves and lairs
underground, as if horror
from the vilest earth,
but no…don't be swayed
by what you've thought or felt,
examine this visitor, alien and slow
but stately, beautiful,
that flows like the earth, twists like the wind
and is alive to here, alive to air,
alive to us.

This is a creature that deserves respect,
magic from somewhere
we've never known, messenger from the dark,
symbol of life and death.
Intruder or guest?
                              I've been told
how to gently pick you up, let you
slide loosely across my hands
and carry you respectfully away.

But I've never touched a snake, imagination
restricts my arms, pushes them back, so
not to touch you or let you touch me.
I'll wait on your retreat to the far trees
where my simian ancestors
rightly learned to fear and hate yours.

Sets His Course

A magpie camouflaged in dazzle paint
among the shadowed foliage,
a transatlantic liner haughty but cautious,
follows his usual track through the garden,

sails the length of the veranda,
as if navigating an outbound coast,
ignores us, old friends often seen
from afar, familiar headlands
to be avoided but never feared.

He sets his course past the kitchen door
where we jettison our food scraps,
fuel for birds and wildlife tramps,
fleets of parrots, convoys of bower birds,
wombats grey and fat as barges.

He gathers up the crumbs, manoeuvres
through the charted reefs and shallows of the shrubs,
and steams for the wide, open sea
across our far-blue, glittering paddock.

Perspectives

Our neighbour's paddock slopes to the road.
On the far side his timber fence
steps down from left to right aslant
our dining room window, against
a curtain of trees, as if theatre flats
had dropped awkwardly on a stage.

The grass looks slopier on the other side,
across our fence, though it really isn't
and the horses enter stage-right
and saunter uphill from our window sill
to the window's opposite corner,
where they level off to graze or stare
placidly ahead as horses do,
at the top of the rise.
                                      It's as if
the horizon has moved closer
to us, as though the earth's curvature
is magnified from my lounge chair
and the distant trees are floating in a green sky.

From the crest of the paddock, looking back,
our house dips to the right and the roof
seems lower there as it nestles
into the hill, but it's also
further from the fence and partly hidden
by our own trees, so what you see,
of course, depends entirely where you stand.

It's odd to walk in our neighbour's paddock,
to see the house from a novel angle,
as others see it, and the horses too,
and wonder who is looking at us,
from what perspective, where and when,
and how we look to them, if they ponder
what they see, to then imagine vainly
what exactly they make of us.

A White Horse

A white horse against the skyline.
Escarpments and the rolling green of hills,
the wilting blue of summer sky
and the trees, disciplined as soldiers,
stand attentive, wary of those high clouds
aimless and wandering from the west.
Eucalypts evergreen and sharp, their leaves
like shields held high against the sun.

In the green and blue, one white horse
skeletoned against a broad slope of grass
and a bright skyline old as flint and breath.
A shadow thrown down by a cloud
and the horse galloping in the shadow.
The mind clicks to now, thinks of tomorrow.

If at First…

Sitting on the rocks in the creek,
our small Jack Russell
leaping from rock to rock,
happily playing around the pools
in the currents of clear water.

Then a huge chasm, the water deep,
but of course, that's
where she had to go.
One leap. She missed,
slid into water, was
scooped up, placed on the rock,

but no, half leapt, half scrambled
back to where she'd started,
looked in that questioning way
dogs have, as if to say,
'What did you do that for?
I'll do it myself, thank you.'

With an even mightier leap,
for a small dog, she was there,
on the rock she wanted to reach,
by herself, unassisted and happy.

Alessandro and the Giant Bird

A wild descent to Yogyakarta,
air brakes raised okay, main flaps useless,
airspeed out of control –
the sickening thump
onto concrete, the slam and slide,
eighty tons of 737 crumpled,
careered off the runway, landing gear shattered,
a bruised and wrenching stop and then
the darkness…

Seat 21, behind the wing,
Alessandro Bertellotti saw
light from the rear door –
in eight steps was out.
He turned to see the wreck erupt in flames.

Blood from his lip but nothing broken
and nothing to be done, Alessandro
caught a cab to town
and went to work.
Bought new clothes, too much blood,
the conference he'd flown in to see,
then took his ticket
back to Yogya airport
and calmly flew to Melbourne, home.

A little nervous on take-off,
either fly now or never fly again,
had a snooze, the next landing was fine.
'I'd like to leave this day behind.'

Garuda, that fabulous bird,
so large it blots the sun,
half-man, half-eagle,
a national symbol.
For dinner in Melbourne
that night
Alessandro ordered chicken.

The Edge of Reality

on Quantum Theory

We're all prisoners shackled in the cave:
we see only shadows reflected on a wall.
No matter how well measured and defined
they're merely reflections of reality,
there, behind us, that we cannot see.

Do the experiment – set it up
to measure particles of light
and you'll get streams of photons
but try to measure waves and you'll get waves –
or step away so nothing's measured,

you'll get neither waves, nor particles
but something else that's always there
and what that is, we've no idea at all.
Is reality tricking us to show
only what we expect to see?

Naked reality seems too weird
to comprehend what drives the universe.
Its mystery is stranger than we know,
perhaps stranger than we can imagine.
The more we learn, the less we understand
as the shadows dance in the firelight.

We know these shadows, it's the light dismays us all.
There's no fault in the intricacy of atoms,
perhaps it's in our minds, evolved for here,
for the shadows on a tiny planet
and not the fabled vastnesses there.

From Nothing

A dismal night, rain in cascades,
grey miseries in a smeared world,
compressed in a folded-into-nothing sky.

The night explodes, jet-burst shock shatters
the clouds, the air an arrow flexed and fired.
A crash of light rays, powered impacts
sweeping down to the world here,
a sudden Airbus bursts from murk, descends
from nowhere into this place of matter,
direct from seeming nothing in the sky.

Constantly, around the nucleus of atoms,
virtual particles, electrons or
positrons, emerge from nowhere,
exist for mind-twisting short periods
then collapse into nothing again.

Energy, particles and galaxies,
constellations, planets, rain and people,
merely quantum fluctuations
in membranes of empty time and space,
temporary, frozen phase transitions left
by pulses of wild inflation, matter
formed from a cloud of nothing.

The mind recoils from vast abstractions –
the energy of empty space,
the final simplicity and symmetry:
nothing.

Space, Matter, Time

'Space tells matter how to move
and matter tells space how to curve.' – John Archibald Wheeler

The strongest edifice
collapses if the foundations
are insecure – the tower's lean,
cracks in the bricks.
Something's wrong.

Newton's Law –
Universal Gravitation –
the force of gravity
between two objects,
always inversely proportional
to the square
of their distance apart –
worked well for two hundred years.

Then precise measurements,
the orbit of Mercury.
It drifted, less than one per cent
of a degree over a century
but it drifted.
A crack in Newton's prediction.
Something's wrong.
The whole edifice collapsed.

Einstein's Special Theory,
Relativity –
the speed of light
always the same, irrespective
of the observer or his motion –
Einstein's field equations,
the geometry of space-time
and the red shift of stars.
A universe that expands forever.

Twenty-four per cent of everything –
dark matter.
Seventy-two per cent – dark energy,
invisible, formless, unknown.
We see four per cent
of the universe as matter.

Cracks
in the foundations,
what we think we see,
what there is,
who we are…

The Goldilocks Zone

Our planet Earth is perfect for us,
not too close to our golden sun,
not too hot for us to live comfortably,
not too cold.
Our gravity is just perfect for us
and our atmosphere
has just the right mixture of gases
for us to breathe easily.
Our sky is a lovely blue
because of our atmosphere.
Such perfection can't be an accident.
There must be a plan.
Our god has created
the perfect planet just for us.
We are unique,
the only life in the universe.

Our moon is just perfect for us,
the Ursine Zone.
It makes perfect orbits
around our dear neighbour,
the red gas-giant, which itself revolves
around two brown-dwarf suns
in a figure-eight orbit,
perfectly designed so for half our day
we boil, which is comfortable,
and gives us energy for the other half
when we freeze refreshingly.
Our gravity rises and falls
so we crawl on our sixteen legs
and use our four wings to soar
through our atmosphere of chlorine,
methane and ammonia, so lovely
in its acid green.
We convert its gases into food
with our six noses.
Our moon's surface is rich
in all the elements that allow
our swamps to grow in all their variety
of red and black.
Our creator has designed
the perfect home just for us.

Vertigo

The careless earth plunges away, staggers
from a cliff into nothing but the wide,
shallow dish of sky where footholds
used to be and suddenly they're gone.

Your breath's smashed to shards.
You're left sprawled across the edge of living.

Somewhere below roads twist into
the blue distance and a house shrinks
to tiny. Cling to what you know,
the human scale that makes life normal.

All stumbles into that one push forward
you never meant to make, soft puzzles
that lured you to the very edge
where everything you know dissolves
into the fierce clutch of air, what's left
so small, a handhold beyond your grasp.

Optimism

It's not a high hill but high enough
to see the ridges fall and roll
down to the valley floor, a distant town
and our house snug in its landscape.

It's not the clouds you notice
but the hollows between the clouds
where sunlight's bundled into shafts
sweeping down, grooving between shadows

and spotlit targets in known precincts,
slanting showers lucid with light,
glowing spears hurled by God's hand
that shimmer into patchwork spaces,

illuminations left when the dour clouds
drift on and the sun's rays pour down.

Parallels Never Meet

Walls of cloud bank parallel the coast,
hover on the curve of the sea's horizon
and profiles of ships anchored offshore,
their bows turned north, in line to enter port.

A narrow park borders the road.
A line of pine trees floating-in the sky,
hung between headlands, the only verticals
to frame the margins of the view.

Waves in ranks, an ocean's serried charge
and incessant collapse against the land,
ramparts rolling across boundaries, frontiers
defended by the slow arc of the beach.

The spray of foam hurled onto the rocks,
swirl and turmoil on the basalt ledges,
its rebellious, low-throated moan –

the sea's constant refusal to conform
to geometry or limits or space.

The Mountain Train

The main line west to the mountains.
From Emu Plains to Valley Heights,
the wide Glenbrook Deviation,
its tunnel a narrow portal
into skyworld, valleys crashing away
as water worms down to the sea,
carves its canyons and builds
hollows in the sky, where vistas vanish,
the end of the world's great fells
of scree and broken crust.

Then the one-in-40s, mile on mile,
upgrade curves and cuttings.
Here the railway clings to the ridge
where towns cling to the road's artery
and trains hiss on contours of steel,
hug the steps of a ladder that
winds into grades and altitude.

Steel stanchions and overheads,
bastions of all direct current
like footsteps that stride one after
the other to an infinity of same.
Power works and transformers, wires
that conduct every electric chorus
of silver multiples, four-car V-sets
that surge upgrade, Katoomba's
clifftop walls, the crumbling tableland,
a fortress of brick and tile.

Roadbed and earthworks, nineteenth century
stations, their petite waiting rooms,
where trains stop obedient to the lines
in timetables, the system's hours and minutes,
all reflect metres above sea level,
the pretty names of villages
where every street slides down to cliffs,
away from stations that guard the gateways
to the world here. Conqueror of ridges,
jagged grades and heights, the mainline
to towns that sprawl across the sky,
that build above the clouds.

Post-traumatic

After the hammer blow,
you still think clearly.
You grasp what's happened,
amplify the starkest details.
You're breathing. You sound normal
as you hear yourself answer questions,

but there's no feeling, nothing. You're
shackled in your empty bloodstream.
Ice thickens in your nerves,
crushes you in the crevasse
you've been hurled into.
Minutes freeze, hours, days.

Then the moment comes
when every neuron screeches.

Recollections

Recollections whine in the wind,
memoirs from the street.
A narrow laneway.
High heels like clockwork.

Like whimsy in a glass,
like sirens in the night,
memories and faces
ghost in the shadows.

A red dress, red shoes.
A grey dawn.
Clouds stream in the sky
like tears.

Stars

My window faces west
across the garden
where the great pine tree stands.
I look directly
through its branches
at my neighbour's window,
the only light I see
in the whole building.

There are clouds
as the sky melts
and evening presses in.
I watch
as other lights come on.
Man made stars
replace the stars
I cannot see.

A Pebble

The sea wind is a hymn,
the great bass note of time.

I shimmer in the sunlight.
In the morning
I glow with the dew.
I sing.
I am a pebble
Shining in the road.

There are many pebbles
but always the one road
and sometimes the wind.

Early Spring

The birds buzz in the futile afternoon,
show today's been lengthened by the sun. Light
floods my study, implies this spring I might
achieve the perfect, overcome the gloom.
The early spring insinuates that soon
your dreams come true, all needs are met. Don't fight
just wrap the prize from winter's deepest night.
It's ripe for taking, now, just hum her tune.

But spring's a whore; her promises are lies.
Solicits her clients for the summer,
street-corner tarts and vacant, steel-burnt skies.
Exhausted songs, hollow time that lingers
past the dregs of Christmas, heat that kills, flies,
the tedium of sweat, wind and embers.

Vapour Trails

A sky of eggshell blue.
Vapour trails of white
spread and wander,
washed from precise
by thin breathing.

The tracks and altitude
of jet planes
and the exactness
of high air.

Ladders for angels
that fade
and huge passings
that can no longer
be seen.

The Waves

Waves roll the sand
onto the beach. A mad wind
flings it off again.

It scatters into space.

The dark before the dawn
is soft and yielding
like the skin below the neck
of the warm woman
I sit behind in the theatre.

The depth of night
after the sunset
is sable and hard.
The hair that tumbles
down her back in waves.

The hours of morning
and of night.
The top of her blouse
covers an evening
of bright, white shoulders.

The wind wraps itself
around the trees and trips them up
in its wild dancing.

Spring Rain

My ears notice
that something's wrong.
I listen alertly
to absolute silence.

The faint hum of crickets
in the distance, perhaps
no other sound at all.

The sky has returned to blue.
The so-much-longed-for spring rains
washed the world and went.

Once a frog jumped
into a pond
but the water
hardly splashed at all.

Silence

There's a sound within the silence
the heel of wind among the gums
and from the tame and muted distance
the creek's abrasive clatter comes.

The knock and sigh of grazing horses,
the cool, exotic chant of birds,
the hiss and sway of subtle grasses
within the silence, felt not heard.

Autumn to May

Autumn
brings cooler evenings,
crisper heat.

Winter
and a desk fan
gathers dust.

Spring
a coffee mug
on the bedside table
all day.

In summer
cicadas pulse in time
to my quiet breath.

A White Mug

on the bedside table,
the cold, black tea

I almost drank
early this morning

before my mind grasped
the complexities of being awake.

The sun drifted
slowly from the east

and settled at noon
on its long westward glide.

Today the changing light
was the sole issue.

Dust motes and sunlight
in the room.

A white mug
on the bedside table,

alone, observant,
objective,

an eyewitness to history
that didn't happen.

The Magician

I sit in the dark with the curtains closed.
The dead are dancing across the room.
Storm clouds swirl like flames in the sky.
Candles burn and the shadows loom.

In the silence and out of the dark
the dead keep dancing across the room.
Leaves are chattering like ghosts in a storm.
Candles burn and the shadows loom.

The rocks are melting beneath my feet.
The dead keep dancing across the room.
The world goes spinning into night.
Candles burn and the shadows loom.

My bloodstream beats to a rhythm of time
though the dead are dancing across the room.
I see the rocks. I feel my blood.
I conjure flames where the shadows loom.

Ghostly

There are ghosts in the shadows of trees,
in the shadows of buildings,
in the empty spaces behind the trains
as they pull out of stations

and run like seasons into the future.
There are ghosts in your memories
and in your hopes and aspirations
and in the shadows that follow you.

They love your body's rhythms, your footsteps.
They sway and swing in the breeze, unknown to you
and they are there when you breath in, breath out,
in every cough and when you sneeze.

They hover around you and are attached
to you by your past, your mistakes
and failures, the threads that bind you
to them. They cling to your life like the air.

Ghostwalking

I live with a ghost, the romance
whose throat you cut when you stormed out
into the night, leaving me alone, numb
in the creeping cold, the realisation
I'd been spat at, insulted, humiliated.
Our relationship lasted a year, perhaps less.
Its corpse was buried in the hissing
emails you hurled at my face, but its ghost
still lingers in my phantom nerves.

No shrieks in the night, no white sheets
or hurtling crockery, just mists
that hover between sleep and the clear light.
The mind succumbs to whatever sad ghoul
floats under its defences, traces
of what I thought I had in voice, in flesh
and blood but now the drama's insipid,
faded into vagueness and white, ghostly
as the frail dawn where Hamlet's father walks,
his spirit's vain searching for the lost prince.

For months, the memory provoked a pain
so real in my guts I thought I'd been kicked.
Post-traumatic, wrenching, hard. I had.

I think of you and see a hollow shade
that drifts into the edges of my day
and all I feel is blank indifference,
but the mornings can still be cold
as I think of you before, a mist that
coalesces into a lone figure,
a deserted stage in an empty theatre, its
mirage of speeches that could have been made
but never were, the script of a play, edited,
crafted, rehearsed, that was not performed then
and never will be now.

Faces in the Sea

Stand in the bow, the night ferry, look down
at the white lips of suicides, at whirlpools
of tossed skulls, grinning, staring back,
skeletons that dance the whispering dark.

Our ship ploughs them under, churns hard water
into foam. Their chains and shackles rattle
against the hull. In our wake, risen voices,
drowned sailors shimmered into mist, glisten

in the starlit fairgrounds of death. The sea
makes a softer boneyard, smothers its missing choirs
where no bodies are ever found, hurls ships
of the living into cemeteries of drift and waves.

The Night

The night is in my eyes,
and beside me.
Numbed by long goodbyes,
the sky's mystery.

The night flies in my face,
sprints ahead of me.
Streetlights' mirage of grace,
their hollow intensity.

The night, the stars, the moon
merge and moan around me.
Morning comes too soon,
the night clings inside me.

The Young Moon

after Sergey Yesenin

Mist is building across the lake.
Paddocks lie bare after harvest.
In the distance, the hills are turning blue
as the sun rolls towards the horizon.

Water seeps into the ruts in the road
which meanders away wearily,
as if soon the world will awake
to the grey-haired reign of winter.

Yesterday I sat among the trees
listening and watching as a bay moon
skipped above the mist and branches
and harnessed itself to the earth and sky.

Dangerous

The moon's held by the Earth's rapture.
Small, enticing in its phases
and its moods, half hidden in clouds,

peaking from its shadow, naked
behind its clothes, which it removes
coyly, monthly, a slow stripper,

seduces the Earth, keeps it loyal
with its light, its glamour, its lure.

The Earth holds it like a mistress,
shy and sweet, who it rarely trusts.

Coalcliff

Neon reptile, the train
burrows through late afternoon.
Half in darkness,
great escarpments
glower down,
flex black, granite muscles,
raise boots
of buttressed clifftops,
ramparts and scree sloping up
then bowing to their gods
of height and sheer
whose bodies parallel
the Illawarra coast,
crowd its thin corridor,
road and rail,
between waves of the sea
and the shoulders of the Earth.

The train scurries on,
shelters in the Clifton Tunnel
like a lizard glowing
in a crack of rock,
hides beside the trackside ruins,
coke ovens,
derelict and cold
that crowd the tunnel's mouth
like rockfall,
until the cliff's slow retreat
to rolling hills,
green valleys
and there are horses
where the world
reduces to human scale
after the land of giants.

Illawarra Dreaming

Waves moan below me.
It's spitting with rain.
I'm surrounded by water.
A gaunt collier's
anchored out to sea.
Port Kembla to the south
and north
a vista of rocky headlands
fades into mist.
Years and distance.

The train skirted the national park,
wooded glens and gullies,
the elegant, crumbling viaduct at Stanwell Park
and the rat-hole Coalcliff Tunnel,
braved the slender passage
between the sea and the cliffs,
space only for the railway and road
through Scarborough.

A few doors from the house
where he wrote *Kangaroo*,
D.H. Lawrence Reserve
slopes to a set of steps
that draw you down
to rocks and a small beach
where waves break
into tantrums of spray and foam.

Near this headland Lawrence conjured
right-wing militias and the pain
of the 1920s,
old politics of remnants and memories.
Here the remains of a wooden jetty
where coal was loaded
into small ships
berthed but still at the mercy
of the open sea –
the great, uncaring, grey Pacific.

The Gardens

I followed the rusted staircase down
to a rock ledge,
where the sea boiled beneath me
and flung squalls of spray

onto the rocks beside me.
I sat and scribbled out
the first draft of
'Illawarra Dreaming'.

I looked out to sea
and up and down the misted coast.
But isn't that just the thing?

We sit at our silent desks
and measure images and metaphors
in stillness and solitude,

gaze out at our mild, moist gardens
while our lives rage beneath us
and the world shatters like a cliff face.

A Suburb

We took the train to an outer suburb.
A bitter, overcast day, midwinter.
walked through the town centre, followed the road
out to the perimeter fence, not far.

Bare, ruined rows of deserted barracks,
small, wooden bunks stacked like racks.
The silence of abandonment and ghosts,
traffic moaning in the distance, the wind.

A museum, no other visitors.
Thousands died here, starved, beaten, gassed,
died of disease or shot, just a short walk,
the station, an outer suburb,

one of the country's largest cities. Ghosts.
Thousands died here. We left, in silence.
A short walk from town, an outer suburb
of Munich, thousands died here, Dachau.

Gliding Home

Leaving Adelaide
minutes behind the red
Virgin Blue 737,
surging into air
out across the gulf,
the tight turn south,
Glenelg hovering
like a fortress on the sea
and curving east,
thirty thousand feet or more,
the whole south-east continent
laid out below
in green and yellow tartan
and there
strange and vapour-soft
skeins like tracks
of seraph's wool
hang in the hollow sky.

An hour or more
we ran that Virgin's
perfect contrails,
tubular and pure
towards our sure
and parallel descent
to warmer airspace,
the grim and gothic
precipice,
the troll-eroded
tablelands,
we arrowed straight,
precisely down
Sydney West Approach,
the angel's railway
gliding home.

Over the Shoalhaven

A mosquito-buzzing drone
brooding eastwards into night.
Cramped steerage in the belly of a Boeing,
waiting as the air miles wind themselves
tediously back to home and morning.
Two a.m. in transit at K.L.
then lightning scours the Timor Sea.

Vectored south of Sydney,
a wide sweep to the morning's ocean flight path,
dipping westward into Kingsford Smith.
A hollow hemisphere of land and space
floating here among the sunburst blue,
a wild clarity of light
crashing into kilometres
of air and height,
the sprawl of endless greeneries,
archaic bush and rock.

A wilderness,
ancient, mysterious and home.
The ribs and shoulders
of turtle mountain Coolangatta.
The blue serpent, thin Shoalhaven
also winds homeward to the sea –
the lifeblood, body and the face
of what and who I am
and where I'm meant to be.

Driving Home 3 a.m.

Roads glisten,
streetlights in the rain.
The yellow glare
of highways.
An emptiness of suburbs.
An envelope of dark.

Drive the lonely highway
in the early hours of morning.
The magnitude of night,
a city of the dead
in the solitude of darkness
life becomes a thread.

Roads glisten,
sunlight in the rain.
The yellow glare
of morning.
A busyness of suburbs.
The envelope of light.

The sun is also rising
on the living
and the dead.

Race the Storm

I drove with the wind
to race the storm.
Pellets of rain
from the great cloudbulk
hung on the black cliffs
and buttressed the sky.

Shells and bullets
shot on the windscreen,
plunging fire spread in sheets.
An artillery of wipers
scattered shrapnel
into ribbons and sleet.

The car split the stormstreaks.
The lurch and toss of the road,
a hum and whine of tyres
sizzled and grunted
against the gust and gales.

The car blurred rain showers.
I ran like a clipper under sail,
storm clouds heaving in my wake
and the horsepower winds
hugged and wrestled
like lovers more hungry
mile after mile.

Driving Home

Driving home every Sunday's a dry ritual.
Two hour's suspense of self and place and time.
It's not weekend. It isn't working week,
those days you fret to organise the world.

It's not the green life – air and animals,
gardens fresh as newsprint, lawns like prairies
in the sun. Read and ponder, play
mad, childish games with the neighbour's dog.

It's just direction – the precise transit
hum of movement, points on maps, regular
as gypsy roads. Leaving home conjures yet

another home. Driving's the long ceremony
before the act. Roads embrace our futures
with rites both formal and exact.

Home

Open the door and it's cool,
everything's neat –
exactly as I left it
and quiet, except
for the rainbow lorikeets,
their shrill conversations
on their branches
next to the balcony,
their home
and this is mine.

I close the door,
turn my back on traffic,
noise, other people
and relax into myself.
I don't need company,
don't need television
or telephones,
just a book,
a CD playing –
this is exactly here,
nowhere's the outside world.

Our House

The house we planned and saved for, furnished painfully
one piece at a time, is now twenty-five years old
and we are a quarter of a century older.
If a marriage survives the first three years, they say,

it's for ever. Today's thirty-four years.
Does that make us safe at last? The wind contorts
the twenty-metre trees, saplings we planted then.
The house stands. Time moves. The house moves through time.

Spirit of Place

A thin, straight fall
down the cliff face.
The creek clatters
away to the south.
The valley softens into meadow
beyond the hills, feeds
to Broughton Creek
and the floodplain.
The wide Shoalhaven
rolls to the sea.

At night, the stars blaze
with a cool, clear intensity
like love
but the landscape
is shaped by water.

A small creek carves
the contours of earthflow,
aeon by aeon, age by age
and the cliffs recede,
high ridge and scar-stone,
tumble-stone and gully,
the interlock and overlap
of downslope. The old escarpment,
backbone of the earth, cradles
shoulders and stomach, hip and thigh,
an amphitheatre of earthscape
scoured from rock, the torso
of the valley floor.
Watercourses, rivulets and streams.
The valley's network of flow.

The house stands
on a gentle slope,
the side of a soft ridge.
Lines of roof, walls of brick,
the columns of uprights
and firm horizontals
in a geology of round,
in the hollows of waterscape.
In winter the sun sets early
behind the escarpment, long shadows
and the comfort of water,
the warm grumbling
of creek-flow in the night.

Rocks and Water

The stones in the creek
are like evidence of shipwreck,
the remains littered, surface remnants
disfigured by water's attention,
greened by moss,
their colours spoiled
by the heat of the sun.

I balance gingerly from rock to rock
as you scamper far ahead.
I search for footholds, sense
the curves of boulders
below my feet,
the slipperiness of slime,
use my hands
to grapple the larger rocks,
almost on my knees,
in fear of my own shipwreck.

I stop, catch my breath, sit clumsily,
watch the current as sunbeams
bounce across clear water,
until you look back with concern,
begin the long trek
downstream, towards me.

I signal Stop!
Dizzy with empty footholds,
I point to the bank,
clamber up the slope,
my feet still slipping
as I hook a sapling,
haul myself to level ground
and there you are
smiling down at me,
as if walking on wet stones
is not a problem for someone
with your normal balance,
then the quick skip along the road.

I feel the sun drying my clothes
but the shade is chill.
I remember the vertigo,
the sideways shove of dark,
a shipwreck of spin and fall,
collapse into swirled abyss.

Then the sun again.
You look at me and smile.
We walk hand in hand,
stable on the road
beside the creek.

'Tramps and Hawkers'

I listened to the song.
The words at first meant nothing
though now I realise
they're quite beautiful.

It was the lilt of the melody
seduced my attention and something clicked,
a new scent, the recognition
of something lost that's almost found.

Glasgow's Battlefield Band,
words from the nineteenth century
but the tunes marked 'Traditional',
celtic, sweet, lyrical and sad.

> *'I'm happy in the summer time*
> *beneath the bright blue sky.*
> *not thinking in the morning light*
> *at night where I'm to lie.'*

Familiar, a tune from long ago,
it tugged at my mind and senses,
a feeling more than a memory, more
an atmosphere of somewhere else, and then:

A teenager, my parent's home,
the Clancy Brothers on LP:

> *'Put on your dungaree jacket*
> *and fasten the belt on your vest*
> *and tell them you're a poor sailor lad*
> *that's been to Paddy Wests.'*

A song of young men lost at sea.
I longed to go to sea but never did,
there may have been salt in my heart
but my life's been lived on dry land.

A tune from my past, different words,
they're Scottish travellers and hawkers now
but fifty years ago, Irish sailors.
All roving lads. I felt the surge

of then and there, sad at the loss of dreams,
innocence withering somewhere among
the words of an old song. I was
seventeen when first I heard it.

Something

Looking through the window onto darkness,
a CD playing, the humidity
of late summer. My desk fan whirs.

As midnight approaches, the night tenses
its transformation into tomorrow.
My watch-face begins to change, circles
into the new day. Across the garden
an outside light's still burning but the moon's
lost somewhere on its lonely orbit.

The graveyard shift, the thin small hours,
when your will's hollow, your soul cold
and your mind's prey to all the ghosts you
thought you'd lost on highways or in whiskey.
Neil Young singing, 'Something's saying something
but no one seems to listen.'

His CD ticks its dark heartbeat,
sweep hands race into tomorrow, you listen
as the night sings the black songs of the world.

Muse

At my desk, soft lamp glow, you my sweet ghost
at my shoulder there naked muse, I write
you quietly into words to the goddess
yet you're a woman real as skin, my tongue
still tastes your memory, shapes your breasts
under my hands. Your voice murmurs below
songs of black submission, music of lust
and magic, my muse, my friend, my lover.

Daughter of Uranus and Gaia, desired
Erato charm my sight with your dark wreathes
of violets and roses, mistress of Eros,
breathe in the glamour of my creation,
naked words on naked paper, you're still
carnal, woman yes, mine and sensual.

Wrecking Ball

My watch face clicks to midnight,
the desk lamp burns, interrogates the room,
my desktop varnished yellow,
shelves and books stacked in columns
and lined paper
littering,
all of it blank.

I wrap myself in music again.
Dylan sings:

> *And how does it feel*
> *to be on your own,*
> *no direction home*
> *like a rolling stone?*

My fingers knot on my memories.
I smell the morning.
I taste my own fear
of the new sun rising
like a ball
thrown at me hard
that I have to catch.

If I don't
it'll drop like a boulder
and roll away
and my life will roll away
and keep rolling.

My Desk

My green banker's lamp
and its warm light.
The plastic desk fan
spins. A neat row
of dictionaries
and guidebooks.

Horizontal slats, cream venetians
and blackness in the window beyond.
The great sky-twisting
pine tree, I know is there
but cannot see,
its branches whirl and its leaves
wind upwards to the moon.
My neighbour's bathroom lights
and the outside doorway lamp
burn with a cold light,
the building opposite,
the other side of the courtyard,
grass and gardens.

I search my desk
and the bars of blinds,
the criss-cross plastic
window ribs.

I search the night
for answers to the white page.

The world keeps spinning out
to midnight.

A Silhouette

A warm desk,
my green lamp
and the blackness
of trees,
beyond the neatness
and geometry
of curtains
and windows.

I sweat
to conjure rhymes
from the blank page,
a labour
from the bowels
of hell

yet sometimes
hatched in silhouette
and haunting the shade,
slips from the shadows
something rare,
something strange.

Angels in the Mind

'…we need to acknowledge
visitations by intense psychological
presences, and that birds are the
closest things we have, more or less,
to angels.' – Robert Adamson

On the balcony watching lorikeets
shrapnel into splintered colours, prisms and
explosions of rainbow, I thought of you
dark angel, Spanish eyes, your nightfall hair
and patient gaze unwavering, direct
in the power of silence, your being
exactly who you are and knowing it,
as shadows know the night, though intimate
with sunlight ignore it, irrelevant and false.

Then suddenly a cacophony of wings, a blast
of cascade air and two huge messengers
in their power and purity all white
like daylight angels dropped from heaven –
two perfect sulphur-crested cockatoos
trailing glamour through a summer afternoon, shrill
as a bride, her train and gown of gorgeous wings,
groomed and radiant. I glimpsed the elegance
in symmetry of nature and the mind:

dark angels haunt reality like ghosts.
Those more blatant voyagers hurled like songs
down from the dazzled sky, colour and light,
enchantments by the obvious and loud,
or the permanence of the old shadows,
still and silent chronicles swept by night,
angels from unseen edges of the moon,
the simplicity of a dream, darker
presences, poised in mansions of the mind.

The Imp

To sit opposite you,
to chat, laugh, wander
through the depths of your dark eyes,
alive to the flow of words,

holding, assessing, warming to me, responding
to my inanities, feelings,
the cut and clarity of your mind.
To hear your voice in the narrative,

your imagination and your knowledge,
the sheer, overwhelming power
of personality and response,
your intelligence and restraint,

but best the little girl who hides
in the complexity of your smiles,
who giggles at cleverness and wit,
especially the rude and vulgar.

She's naughty and she's wise. She's there,
daughter of banter, mystery
of the perfect lady and the brat,
the child of your jokes and certainty,

who tumbles like a water sprite
along the cascade of your mirth.
You're elegant, intense and beautiful
but it's not hard to see the imp in you.

Special

I knew you were special
the first time
I saw you.

As we walked home
you took my arm
in the brilliant night.

We danced naked
in a small room
full of clothes.

One autumn we met
in an empty bar
and I never saw you again.

The great Earth still swings
on its lonely track
through time and space,

and I still
think you're special,
more so now.

Whatever Remains

I went back to the place
I'd met you, where I kept meeting you
for years.

It hadn't changed. It was as if
I'd never left. I felt
instantly at home.

I kept thinking of you
but didn't conjure you there.
No ghosts appeared.

I didn't detect your perfume
nor perceive your face.
I couldn't imagine your voice.

The building remains
as it always remains.
We come and go,

go…pass into memory.
There are no ghosts.
All that happens is now.

Autumn 1994

for Maree Samueljan

A summer of bushfires and death,
your death, by truck, on Mount Ousley.
An autumn of leaves and illness.
I tried to find your grave and failed,
too soon. No headstone then to mark
that dismal row, and drove for solace,
numb and shocked with disappointment,
I parked in a street of weeping trees.

One perfect leaf, broad, dry and brown,
wedged between the wipers and the screen
like a virus, the beauty and the loss.
That autumn I drove towards collapse.
My nerves quivered with the fluttering
of leaves and the cold commotion of ghosts.

Great Rainbow, Dad

My father was an expert
on colour printing – best
in the country.

His world, his working life,
was a nuance of colour,
its composition and its flow –
his bloodstream, heartbeat
and his taste, his sense of smell,
the radius of his eyes.
Cunning in colour, a magician,
he hauled the delicate
hues from black, from white,
lifted shades to scarlet, shadows
into magenta, golds that spiralled
like worlds
away from the sun.

He sifted, painted, wove and shaped.
The rainbow burned
on his page,
printed and imprinted –
the eyes of swirl,
spectrums in midnight
and the dance of photons
every dawn,
cones and rods,
retina and lens,
his daylight in his everyday.

The afternoon of his funeral
a thunderstorm in monotone –
banks of grey on sheets of dark
and black across the sky,
sucked the colours
from the morning.
Rain in broadsheet fell
mired like midnight on the sun…

and then the rainbow
like a resurrection
vivified the sky –
a gift from Dad to say goodbye.

Gosford Hospital, 2 a.m.

The corridors are like an empty breath.
A coiling away of lights, linoleum
and carpet merged to distance, doors
threading a maze. Fluorescent numbers
arrow into space, signpost the words
of sickness, infection, death: Critical,
Coronary, Surgical – all sterile
and precise in print and place.

The morning's small hours when no one moves.
Lights descend like disinfectant
and silence seeps like a bandage.
Casualty's night attendant unlocks
an electronic door, the secret codes
of healing. Turn right, move across the face
of stairs, skirt the close-mouthed smirk of lifts
dangling like the eyes of patients
left somewhere sleeping in the night.

Another door. Give a name, then face
the nurses' station and the ward.
My father's numb, unconscious breathing.
Tubes of plastic, the wretched, swollen
grasp for air, his groping snatch at life.
Lungs deliver just enough to struggle through
each grate and cycle, then to face the next.

Twisted hands, gnarled and bandaged wrists,
tubes that fly away to pumps,
blinking numbers counting the litres,
nourishment, air forced panting past his tight
and withered lungs. A mask strapped to grimace,
his face deadened as some actor, not
the man I know, plays this dying role,
a cruel theatre's stark and new, apparent
late and final act.

I move to ease the pressure on his nose,
touch his forehead. His breathing boils
through my fingers. The son who almost died
urges his father's gasping into calm,
wills the oxygen to spark his life again,
ignite to a full and normal sleep,
as once, his pre-term son was willed
to love the air, to breathe again and live.
I say to my father, 'Just keep on breathing…
keep on breathing,' half a century, more,
since my young father whispered that to me.

My Father's Rainbow

Sheets of rain paint a rainbow into life.
The sun braids parallels and bands of splurge
against the pallor of clouds on the verge
of a ghost-lit palette, the brush and knife.
Grey clings to black in the thunder's strife.
Lightning sizzles to green, a sky-mad surge
in the brilliance of the storm, the high curve
of cloud banks castling into spray and spite.

His rainbow spins with furrows of cold light
as my father once wove shades and colours,
this morning his funeral in the floral garden,
when the sky was clear and the sun was bright.
I see the arc as a badge of honour
and take those hues as his gift from heaven.

Haunted

for Maree Samueljan

You died in summer.

In the autumn
I drove to the cemetery again
to say goodbye
and couldn't find your grave.

A brown, fallen leaf
had wedged
between the wiper blade
and the windscreen.

I couldn't touch it.

All that May
I drove mesmerised,
my nerves fluttering
with ghosts.

For Destruction Ice

A black wound to your soul.
I've touched your scar and tried
but cannot reach with words
where some bright angel died.

Slow glaciers of pain
grind in your damaged heart.
I cannot navigate those seas
ice floes tear apart.

You slip from me in fear,
you who I cannot hate
and the ice around your heart
is black and hard as slate.

Hard and cold the roof
on the cottage built of stone
though slate is best to shelter
the hearth, the heart, the home.

A Touch

I was worried you were ill
but had never before seen fear
shatter your face and kill
the spirit there.

My fragile more-than-friend,
I watched the reptile pain
hollow your eyes and rend
their brightness. In vain

the instinct comfort,
as if intensity could ease
your misery with a thought
a desperate get-well, please

In a thin gesture of despair
my hand was on your shoulder,
a shield no stronger than air
as your courage grew colder.

My hand meant nothing then
and my words mean little now,
just the impulse to defend,
if only I had the power.

Six Months Later

It's late autumn.
A grey,
repentant sky.

Leaving my door
I stop to zip up
my jacket
against the wind and rain
once more.

I walk
the same narrow path
through the parks,
across the playing fields,
the deserted golf links
and the roads…

I watch the same river run
resignedly
down to the sea –
it's a different month now,
there's no you,
there's just me.

Ern Malley's Children

The ghost of Ern Malley shrieks to the moon.
Geometry's prison, brickwork and tile,
a neatness of lawns, a darkness of smiles
that moulder to secrets locked in old rooms.
Blue eyes and staring and vacant with ruin,
yellowing faces, infected with bile,
with madness, racism, conformity's style.
There's acid in verbs, the. stockmarket booms.

The ghost of Ern Malley shrieks in the sun,
jibbers and moans, condemned to a poem,
he shivers in shadows, lurks within words.
Prophets and sibyls from the suburbs may run,
prayers and portents etched in their vowels
but lyrics of failure cut like a sword.

Common Sense, Really

My work colleague says I'm a funny man,
an actor. She teases and delights, laughs
when I agree with her. 'The coffee's cold
and it's all your fault!' I say 'I'm sorry' and look
mock-repentant. She claims its a tactic
that just deflects attack. She could be right.
But I hope its more a skill to make life
easier to take. Why react to nothing?

Jokes enliven the day and ease the pain
in rubbing up against someone else. There's
many a war's been won avoiding battles.
Shock and awe stuns from someone slow to act.
Only fight if your human core's attacked
and if you have to, then you fight to kill.

Malvolio Again

Yes, I've inflicted and I've suffered pain,
injected morphine and I've held the lash,
cringed beneath their soul-skinned, broadside wordfire,
chainshot, sniper's fire, pug-faced punches thrown.
In Observatory Park I sat stunned,
exhausted, numb and taut with stress, surveyed
the Pyrmont skyline and my life. Felt the end.
Then four months lost, my life drained, virus bled.

A goddess I was awestruck with, riding coat
in black, long, bare legs, spoke to humiliate, spat
her spitfire words. I've heard her daughter say
she's lost all speech. Inwardly I rejoiced –
time's whirligig had brought his twenty years'
revenges in. I'm glad I used the lash.

Diligence

My class works silently on the task I've set,
absorbed in their writing, dictionaries
open on each desk, their youthful lives spent
in listening, research, in learning and in chat.
I wonder how they think of me – mentor
gentle, greying, kind, I hope. My younger colleagues
say I'm wise, quick-witted, funny, a link
to other generations and their older ways.

But I'm a husband, brother, poet too.

I'm ribald, staid, monotonous and wild.
I've stood behind a bound, naked woman
and swung the cat o'nine tails at her back.
I've travelled, suffered, cried and dropped down drunk, always
been an actor, diligent in the roles I've played.

Choose Your Ground

A work colleague
looked at me seriously, said,
'When there's a disagreement
you always get your way. How?'

I thought about that,
said to her, 'Nine times out of ten
I couldn't care less what happens,
I go along with everybody else,

But Number Ten, if I'm sure,
I'll dig in my heels, make a stand
and everyone notices.'
The moral is, Be reasonable.

If you want to get your way,
fight only the battles you choose to fight.

Stormcloud

Flexed, bowstring taut,
the air ratchets up to tense,
tightens nerves, notches
into dank. Sodden with heat,
swamp-claws swell
to stress and soak, oil and sweat
oozes from your pores.

Look up and see
great black columns
of crossbow clouds.

Naptha flares,
windsquall-shattered marshlight
and the campfires
of stormtroops.

Grim archers tighten
their longbows, shafts of steel
and arrows volleyed,
the cold, clean tips of raindrops
feathered by a crisp
damp-slaughtering wind.

Leaves in the City

Brown feathers, arid kites, batter themselves against
solid corners, obedient only to
the commands of the wind, the song

of hollow air that erodes sharp edges,
smoothes away the clarity of here, blurs
precision of place in its mad sprinting

somewhere else, seduces leaves with its breath,
then abandons them to the hard world
of poverty, litter and decay,

like a false lover, suave with words and smiles,
bounteous with gifts and airy promises,
the full blast, whirled-away, no breathing left.

Fallen leaves, full-blown vagrants,
trespass through the doors of restaurants,
cringe away under the brooms of waitresses.

Milkman

The slow clip, clop
of the milkman's horse.
The clatter of glass
early in the morning.
His slow approach along the street
and the squeal of our front gate.

Normally, two or three full bottles
left at the front door
for Mum to collect.

For days
holes in the tinfoil tops,
an inch or two of milk missing
and the mystery of how and who.
At first, we suspected tramps
until awoken
by the chatter
of magpies drinking.

Rowena

Rowie for us was almost
a private waitress. A little
far-away, self-contained, as if
only there because she chose to be
but always a presence, she ran
the coffee-shop as mid-Victorian schoolma'ams
ruled their single teacher schools.

Rarely made small talk, Rowie
stopped to chat with us but never
slow to serve the others.
Efficient, organised and calm,
she got very curt with those
she thought unreasonable,
demanding or simply not polite.
Remembered our usual orders
better than we did and once
put me politely in my place
when confusedly I questioned
what she'd brought. I wasn't thinking
but expertly she was.

She served us every Saturday,
were sometimes quite upset if she
dared to take a weekend off
and wasn't there for us. Always
agreed on politics – the sheer
awfulness of Howard's
right-wing government. Shrewd, incisive
comments and her philosophy of life.
She easily became for us
an equal and our friend.

Late thirties. A striking, oval face
and blonde hair smartly tied a ponytail.
Slim, demure and dressed in black.
I really found her very sexy
though never dared to mention that,
especially to my wife.

We learned about her daughters, one
teenage, the other younger. She'd
pushed away a messy, pointless marriage
but somehow found the time to study
and almost finished her degree.

Tripped at work and smashed her foot.
A nasty fracture, slow to heal,
at home for months on compensation,
she soon decided never to return
and went to full-time uni after that.
Good for her. The strong, intelligent
and sharp don't need to spend
their lives in taking breakfast orders
or in serving food to strangers.
But jeez, since she's been gone
breakfast at the Berry pub
has never been as good.

Long Black Hair

A little girl running home
at lunchtime or after school
and sometimes we exchanged
a few words
but I seem to remember
she was always running,
disappearing through the gates
of the flats
I passed every day,
halfway between school and home.
They're still there
fifty-five years later.

I was fascinated
and perplexed.
I didn't know why –
the elusive female even then –
desirable somehow, enigmatic.
I was ten years old.

At the end of the year
we sold our house
and moved away
to start a different life.
I never saw her again.

I can't remember now
what she looked like,
except for her long black hair.
I've never forgotten that.

Why have the women I've loved
over half a century
all had long black hair,
like the little girl
I remember even now
running home,
the illusion of innocence,
a dream from a lost world
and the reality of a memory
that hardly seems
to have happened at all.

No Ordinary Lunch

Drive from Berry to Bateman's Bay,
then the twists of the mountain road,
the wide, open skies, clouds and space,
lengthened vistas and the high plains.

Stop, as always, for a late lunch
at the art gallery, gift shop, café
in Braidwood and sit comfortably
beside the glass, sliding doors.

Admire the lawn and the gardens behind
and the old, brickwork stables, new
restored, a small, prim residence,
intimate, almost a doll's house.

Notice the dignified lady, a shock
of white hair, leave the house, walk towards us
and try the door beside my wife,
who smiled, moved her chair, apologised,

exchanged the niceties of good manners
with a stranger. I stood in awe –
recognised her at once, her photographs
in books, asked, 'Do you know who that was?'

We'd studied her at school and university,
titan of the century's poetry.
I'd taught so many of her poems, pure magic.
Judith Wright had passed briefly through our lives.

Waiting for Discharge

You're up, showered and dressed,
last night's operation
a success. There's no pain.

Out the window,
a neat suburban street. Normality.
Early morning's stillness.

Sit, wait for the doctor,
so you can go home.
It's cold – wrap yourself
in hospital blankets
as the morning wears on
and nothing happens.

Better than yesterday –
the ambulance, the pain.
Emergency at 3 a.m. Wait.
Wheeled to the CAT scan,
wait, wheeled back.
NIL BY MOUTH in huge letters
above your bed.

Constant pain. Wait.
Shots of morphine.
The operating theatre, 7 p.m.,
wait again, then nothing.

Weird dreams on recovery –
a vague consciousness
of a room
in the dark hole of my head
like a Ted Hughes poem.

And here, wait again.
At least there's no pain
and breakfast, the first food
in three days,
a taste of wonderful normality.

Eighteen Kilometres

Careering south
past the Mount White turn-off,
a hundred and ten, hundred and twenty.
A maelstrom of thoughts
tossed around my head.
My elderly mother.
My frail father left behind
struggles to maintain his breathing,
the pneumonia
that almost killed him.
The hospital at midnight,
the oxygen machines.

I'm looking forward to home,
my own neat bed.
Stress, anxiety and worse
the mind-numb static pace
my family lives
I just can't slow
enough to share.
The last, steep descent
towards the Hawkesbury River Bridge.

I'm wondering
when I'll cross the river…
A roadside exit sign
exclaims Berowra. Where?
The last ten minutes… Where?
No memory of bridge or river,
headlands, cliffs – no thought
of what I'm doing,
how or why.
Eighteen kilometres driven
and no trace
imprinted on my brain,
a curtain closed,
some tedious, clichéd play
I can't recall at all.

And in the courtroom drama,
cross-examination
of my life –
some polished silk
who'd crush my credibility –
an eyewitness but
not to be believed.
Well-intentioned, yes,
but from that distance,
at that speed
and in that light?
Where's evidence to prove
he travelled eighteen kilometres
fast and safe?
And what could have happened,
if it really happened
there
or anywhere at all?

Jervis Bay

I woke to a ballet of waves today
and walked the black meridian of sand
towards the new day just to stand
and watch the sun revive the sleeping bay.

Tentative in silver, ribbons of light
glimmered from the blue. The ancient moon
reflected ripples in the dawn and soon
movement flickered sea stars, cold and bright.

Sunrise dancers flamed the dim horizon,
beamed in a red and yellow firebird's nest,
while spikes of sunlight shimmered wavelet crests
and morning's debut chorused in the sun.

Lives

Early autumn sun,
mid-morning.
The moan and roar of traffic
beyond the window,
in the background,
suggests other lives,
other places
and movement there,
willing or unwilling.

There are wars
and there are refugees,
there is poison,
knives and blood.

My class writes quietly
of love and death
and I contemplate lives
I hope
they never have to live.

Then and Since and Now

Searching for the house my parents
almost bought fifty years ago,
I thought I'd recognise the street
it should've been, almost the spot
it could've stood but wrong and wrong –
nought remains of what I thought
was there, but isn't now, my memory twisted
by the Once, overlain with Since.

Facts corrode forgotten seasons,
a million heartbeats, decades after Then.
Years cascade into cycles of rain and sleep.
The warp of timbers and the rust
of precision, melt your sharpness
into platitude and fuzz,
disconnect the exact
from what is here and now.

Memoirs give way to narratives
and myth, history reconfigures
to a legend in the mind, phantoms
and foundations synapsed so tightly
into fact that Then receded
gently into Wrong.

Waiting

A temporary desk
piled less than neatly
with files and papers,
the fifth and highest floor
of a building
we only partly use.

Part of every day
I teach the classes
almost at the end
of academic courses,
then the final closure
of the college
and my work's
all finished here.

Below me
workmen hammer and paint,
rebuild, remodel,
renovate,
the floors we used to
but no longer use.
Another school
is starting there
different students,
different staff of course,
and purposes different
though similar
to our own.

I feel no need
to decorate or organise
my desk –
it's only where I'll be
a few months more
and why pretend
its permanent.

I sit
and once again
enjoy the view
to the south and west,
the coolness, quiet and space
of this old building
I've somehow come to love
but won't be mine
much longer –
and really isn't mine
in any sense
at all
but just the place
I work.

I watch descending escalators
of planes,
the whole queue
on late approach
to Kingsford Smith –
their flight paths
skim the inner west,
my home and habitat.

I watch the buildings
and the trees
in Chippendale.
I watch the clouds
and the setting sun,
I watch the sky
and wait.

Hear and Do Not Hear

It's not the striking of the bell
in the cold, silent room.
It's the echo that lingers
and the sounds you never hear.

It's not the thing that's done
but the echoes of what was done
that linger in the mind.
They hang in the silent air,
in the later lives of those
who do not listen or will not hear.

The whine of twin-jet
Pratt and Whitneys spooling up
to keep that Boeing in the air –
a final approach on water
before its landing here.

I hear the end of fourteen hours
they've spent hanging in the air,
the echoes of bells were striking
for the passengers up there
and the echoes that brought them here.

Make the decision, buy the tickets,
board the plane and sit and sleep
in a kind of nowhere, never-land,
a kind of slow ringing in the air.

At last through the tiny window
first the water, then the landing lights appear.

I hear the whine of turbines
in the air above this room.

I do not hear the echoes
or the chimes that always linger
in the lives of all those people
that plane was bringing here.

A Problem of Intelligence

John Howard reminisces

No reason to apologise.
We did the right thing anyway
but our intelligence was faulty.

Thousands of Australians marched in the streets
to tell us not to do it
but we went to war anyway.
No reason to apologise.
Our intelligence was faulty.

Every idiot knows that if you start a war
you can't predict the consequence.
but we started this one anyway
In '39 we went to war
to save Poland from the Nazis
but in '45 we gave it to the Russians.
When you go to war
you can't predict the way it ends

but we went off anyway
to save the Viets from the Reds,
to fight the commies over there
and not in the streets of Brisbane.
I guess our intelligence was faulty then.

We went to war in 1914
because…because…well, our allies all were going
so we went too
and changed the world forever
perhaps not entirely for the better
but our intelligence as usual was faulty.

When we invaded Iraq,
half a million people died
and we achieved, well, ISIS, civil war,
terrorism, other wars in Syria and Afghanistan,
collapse in Egypt, Turkey, Libya and Yemen.

Perhaps we didn't find
any weapons of mass destruction
but what does it matter anyway
as we achieved so much.
What was his name again?
The small dictator we overthrew
No reason to apologise
for the Coalition of the Killing.
Our intelligence was faulty.

We did the right thing
so half a million people died.
I don't intend to apologise
because my intelligence is faulty.

Conservatives Rule Okay

The conservative view would be so cool –
just reject outlandish change.
Votes for women! Free the slaves!
Marriage for gays! Madness! Idiocy! Misrule!

It's God, Queen and Country makes me drool.
Never change the status quo!
End of civilisation! Death of order!
Yes the conservative view would be so cool

if only after twenty years and later
you didn't always look a total,
complete and bloody fool!

The Future and Bone

Ghosts in the spine
and feathers of fear.
Late winter and tears
in the sky, on the wind.
The past gnaws at your nerves,
a long memory
of talking to stones.

Russian dolls
coil inside each other
like the envy of angels,
who hold you down
with their wings.

In every city street
traces of forgotten empires,
lost in the cracks.

Behind facades
ancient evils flex
their mad muscles,
flirt with the shadows
in bone canyons
and rise
burning in blue light,
infections spreading diamonds
on a skeleton.

The future tingles
with words like sugar
on your tongue,
the present poised
on a thin ridge
flutters in the wind.

After the long climb
towards today,
sweat in the eyes stings like the sea
and salt tears
taste nothing like honey.

The Mirror

The mirror shows
a different person now.

For years,
fair hair,
then pepper and salt,
now grey,
a steel colour,
bland, uninteresting

and not much of it.
Cut it short
for comfort in summer.

But sometimes
as if to compensate,
the mirror shows me
grey turning white.

One day I'll find
a white-haired
distinguished gentleman
in there,
if the mirror
decides…

I'll find myself
in there
somewhere…

Left and Right

I walk the road
between our neighbour's paddock
and the creek,

drive the highway
between the valley and the coast,
down the escarpment,

ride the main western line
between the mountains
and the plains,

take the bus
between the desert
and the sky.

Roads wind along,
not over, not towards,
always between.

How to Break the Law in Ten Easy Steps

Have pity for people who are suffering.
Think about what it feels to be them.
Decide that the situation must change.
Realise that you must help change it.
Get a visa, board a plane.
Visit the suffering and give them medical supplies
and other necessities.
Listen to their stories and write them down.
Return to Australia.
Talk to the press.
Tell them what you saw.

Parents

My parents rarely argued.
I remember clearly only the one
about selling the house Dad loved
and moving back, closer to Mum's parents.

My mother was calm, ladylike,
rarely lost her temper, but she could be
deeply stubborn, quietly rigid,
immovable as the bank she worked for.

My father was more romantic,
poetic, as a younger man wilder,
but also patient, understanding, wise
by nature and necessity –

the dour certainty of Mum, her parents,
their English, class-driven intransigence,
decades thick, that yearly wore him down.
They chiselled him

into smooth conformity.
An excellent Father, promoted
steadily at work, did well
but never wrote his poetry.

I'm quietly determined like my mum,
sensuous and sensitive like my dad.
Their one mistake affected me
for years – when I was ten

took me away to a lesser suburb,
a different school, that opened my mind
but lacerated my feelings
and retarded my growth

into confidence and humanity.
I can say it now, years after he died,
my father was right but lost the only argument
that really mattered.

It Could Have Been Here

A shopping mall, mundane
as a thousand others, lights too bright,
music too loud, hard metal surfaces
that reflect the names of shops
I'll never use or need.
I've walked tree-lined streets, new apartment blocks,
strolled up the ramp to here…stopped, slightly dazed
at being here…perhaps exactly here…
this clean, transformed, remediated spot.

Spin the insane clocks and calendars
that reverse through decades and shift
fifty years into the past…I'm still standing here…
a student working the long vacation,
dark January…wearing never white,
never clean overalls, that chafe like grit, work-boots,
a hard-hat…sweating the over-sweet, humid air,
among a maze of pipes and tanks, steam and steel,
brick, brown-smeared factory walls.

Three a.m., the graveyard shift, time
to drop the Crystalliser, once per shift
or twice, if you're dead unlucky –
thirty minutes hard, physical labour
high in the steelwork mesh of gangways and pumps –
break up the thickened crust of Sorbitol
so the load empties itself down the cylinder
to liquid vats, twenty feet below.

Really unlucky and it's an hour's work, two men
bent over shovels, sweating, cursing…slice,
push the vile swill, use your muscles, your will,
plead for the hardened slime to break away
into a fat, thick, sewage sludge.
Then stand for eight hours, work a centrifuge,
fed from the same vat, now over your head,
whirl it, scrape the sediment away to fill
metallic drums that took two men, my size,
to grapple out to somewhere else.

Three months rotating shifts – bundy on at seven,
work till three, or three to eleven,
or the zombie hours of morning shift –
eleven at night to seven the next morning.
Crawl out dazed into early morning mist,
home to a drugged sleep, as the other world
wakes to the new day and normal lives.

Some men were glad to sign for double shifts,
overtime and sixteen hours straight, but never me.
The place stank with the sweet, sick stench
of liquid sweetener, different stages of
processed obscenity that soiled my skin
for weeks when I resurfaced to the world
and the new academic term began.

I stand, admire the newness of the mall,
its colours, the shops, the cleanliness, all of it.
I balance modern crassness with the old and vile,
decide against the past and make my way
with pleasure to Hobbyco gleaming over there.

The Greenland Colonies

for Robert Dickins

'In the western settlement
stands a church named Sandnes
that was the cathedral and the bishop's seat.
Now the skraelings* have it all.'

Thus wrote Ivar Bandarson,
the loss of Greenland's second town,
1350 thereabouts.
The death of the last Greenland bishop
1378 and Norway sent
no new bishop then.
The last ship sailed in 1410.
A woman's dress in Herjolfnses churchyard
might be as late as 1430.
The end of Gardar, Hvalsey Church
and then there's nothing.

Societies vanish and leave only questions.
The mystery of how and why –
the farm beneath the sands,
the ruins in the jungle,
the great stone faces.

* Skraelings – lit. 'wretches', Inuits, Eskimo

I think of easily eroded, fragile soils
that can't support the European farm.
The damage done by sheep and cows.
Whole forests cut for timber so
the wind clawed their topsoil into sand,
the remnants cut for turf
for roofs or burning, timber then
too scarce to use.
The heavy load of Christian churches,
conservative and loath to change.
Their vestments, metal and the wood
they wasted, the space and deadweight
in tiny ships, all needed to import.

Their visceral hatred and mistrust
of native Inuits, the Norseman's flat
distaste to learn survival skills from them.
Their only export ivory,
the tusks of walrus so dangerous to hunt,
that Europeans soon disdained,
the Arctic seas so rich
with fish the Viking farmers
never learned to catch, for fishing
means you have to build the boats but boats
need timber and all the trees had gone.

Climate change, the fjords iced up.
The Little Ice-Age started as
the Vikings and the farmers starved to death.
They froze and weakened, dropped
in skirmishes with Indians
and vicious brawls among themselves
for land, for heat, for food.
The last ship sailed from Greenland
in 1410 and then there's nothing.

I think of climate change and fossil fuel,
how Australia once, we're told, rode
triumphant on the backs of sheep
and needed only wool to keep us rich.
The inland turns to drought and dust,
the rivers cease to flow and then
the population flocks towards the coast.
I see the Greenland ice shelf, polar sheets
of continental, mile-thick Arctic ice
melting and the seas rise up.

European culture in that harsh
and far off, strange and alien land,
the Norse, the Viking Greenland settlements,
five thousand people,
lasted almost half of that millennium,
then, nothing.
Australia's bicentenary
was less than twenty years ago.

www.ingramcontent.com/pod-product-compliance
Lightning Source LLC
Chambersburg PA
CBHW070909080526
44589CB00013B/1240